Deaf Culture Fairy Tales: A Companion Coloring Book

By Roz Rosen

Illustrated by Yiqiao Wang

First Edition, January 2017

Written by Roslyn "Roz" Rosen

Illustrated by Yiqiao Wang

Published by Savory Words Publishing
www.savorywords.com

© 2017

All rights reserved under international copyright conventions. No part of this publication may be reproduced or transmitted in any form or by other means, electronic or mechanical, including photocopying, recording, or any other information storage and retrieval system, without the written permission of the publisher, except in the case of brief quotations or excerpts embodied in critical articles or reviews. No page in this book may be photocopied or duplicated in any form.

ISBN 978-0-9863552-7-1

Printed in the United States of America

To my wonderful parents and first teachers,
Ruth Katzen and Abe Goodstein

and

My beloved family: my husband Herb,
and our children, Jeff, Steve, and Suzy

FOREWORD

"As long as we have deaf people on earth, we will have signs. It is my hope that we will all love and guard our beautiful sign language as the noblest gift God has given to deaf people."

George Veditz

This coloring book is a companion to the book *Deaf Culture Fairy Tales*, a collection of classic fairy tales, fables and some songs, with a Deaf-centric twist. *Deaf Culture Fairy Tales*, written for kids ages 1-101 and people from all walks of life, is a book designed to entertain, captivate, and introduce readers and storytellers to different ways of living and loving. This book is available from Savory Words Publishing at www.savorywords.com.

In addition to my husband and family whose endless well of support enabled me to write this book, I want to thank Yiqiao Wang, who enchanted the book with her marvelous illustrations, my daughter Suzy Rosen Singleton for creating the story "The Tortoise and the Hare," and the T.S. Writing Services team. I know you will enjoy the stories and pictures as much as I did writing them and Yiqiao did illustrating them. My appreciation and admiration also go to our Deaf community, with its boundless heritage and linkages.

Roz Rosen
January 2017

TABLE OF CONTENTS

iv	Foreword
3	*Little Red Riding Hood* Little Red Riding Hood and her mother bid farewell to each other using the "I love you" sign.
5	*The Ugly Duckling* With a belt to prevent signing and thus unable to fly south, Ugly Duckling is stuck in the ice.
7	*Snow White* As Snow White enters the cottage, the dwarfs ply her with questions.
9	*The Three Little Pigs* The pigs happily sign HOME and STRONG to the frustrated Big Bad Wolf.
11	*The Princess and the 20 Mattresses* Princess, astonished by how high the stack of mattresses is, signs, "Amazing!"
13	*The Tortoise and the Hare* The tortoise wins the race with the help of captioned glasses and an interpreter amulet.
15	*The Little Mermaid* The Little Mermaid confesses in mime to the Prince that she saved his life.
17	*Hansel and Gretel* Hansel and Gretel enter the House of Goodies, unaware that the shingles on the roof are from children who at one time signed.
19	*Beauty and the Beast* Beauty is awestruck by the dazzling visual symphony created by Beast in his music room.
21	*Phoenix* As a result of Mom signing to her baby, Phoenix rises again!
23	A to Z: Daactylology

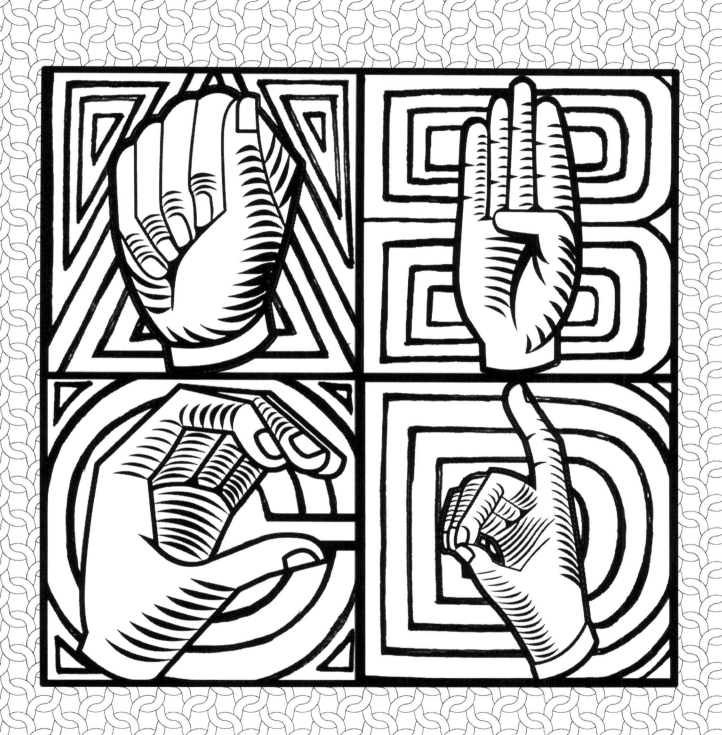

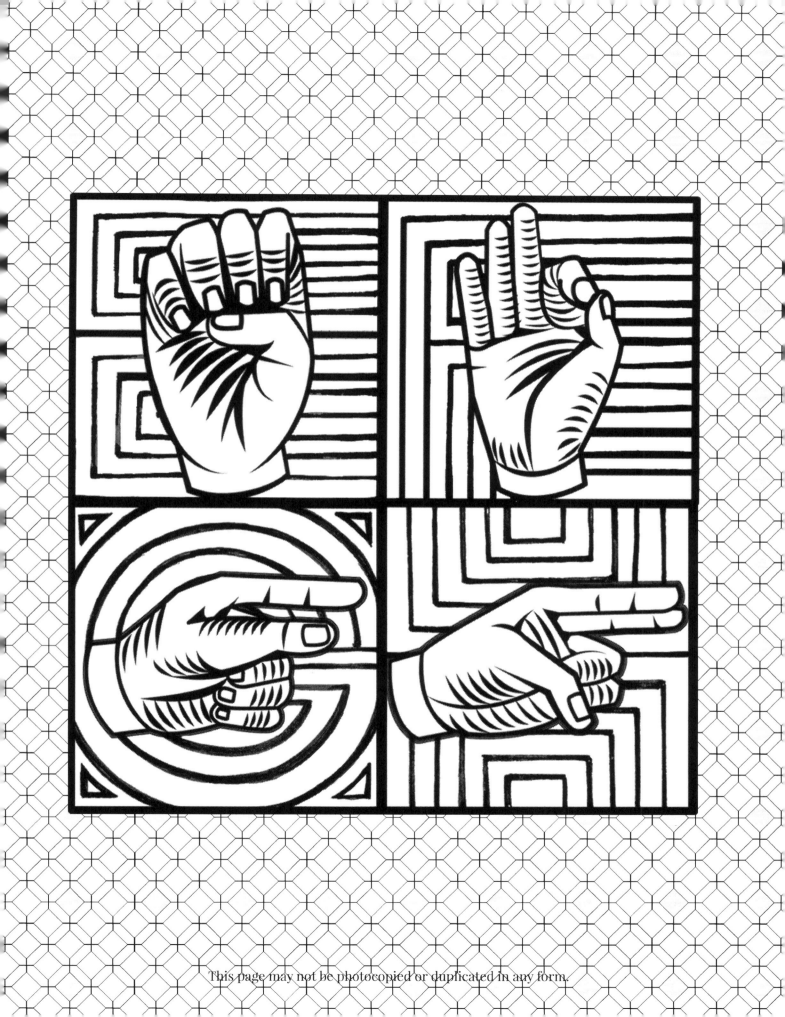

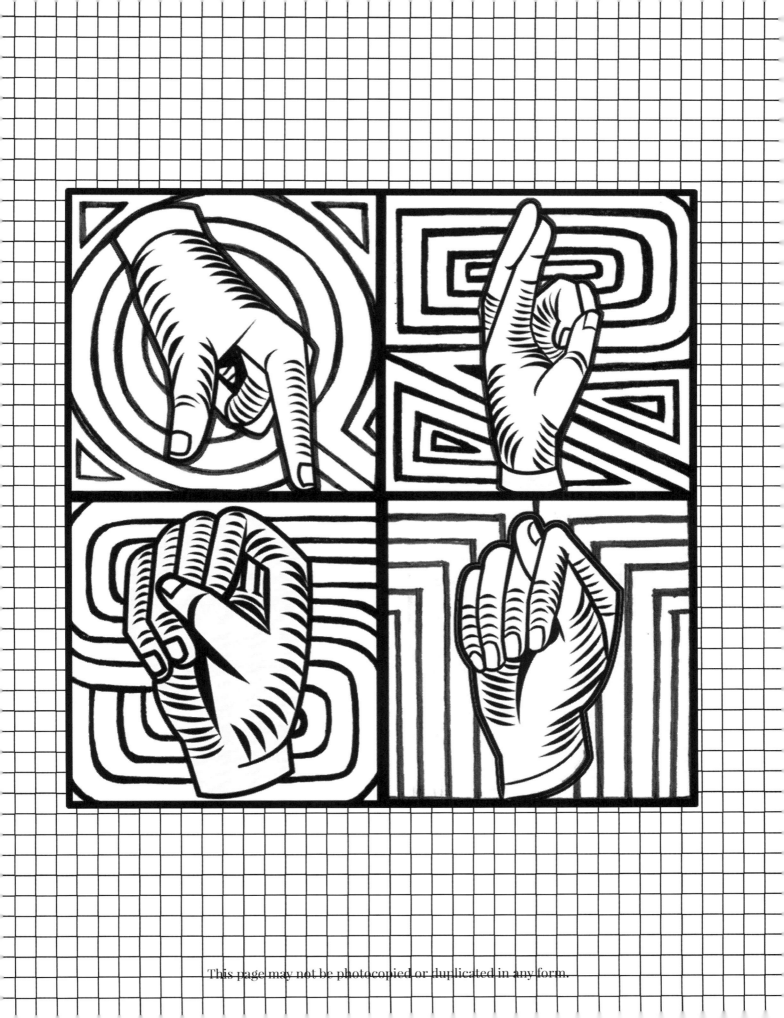

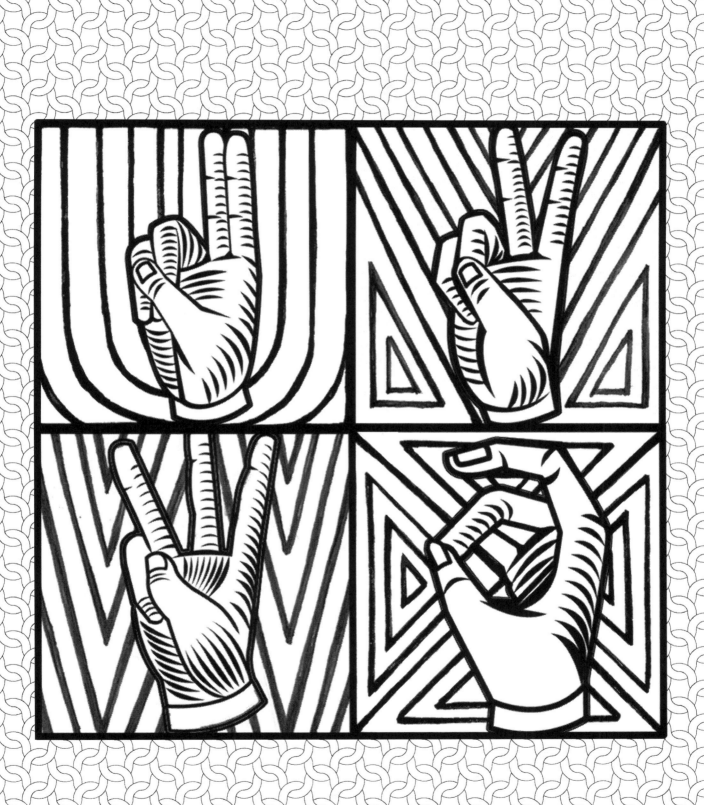

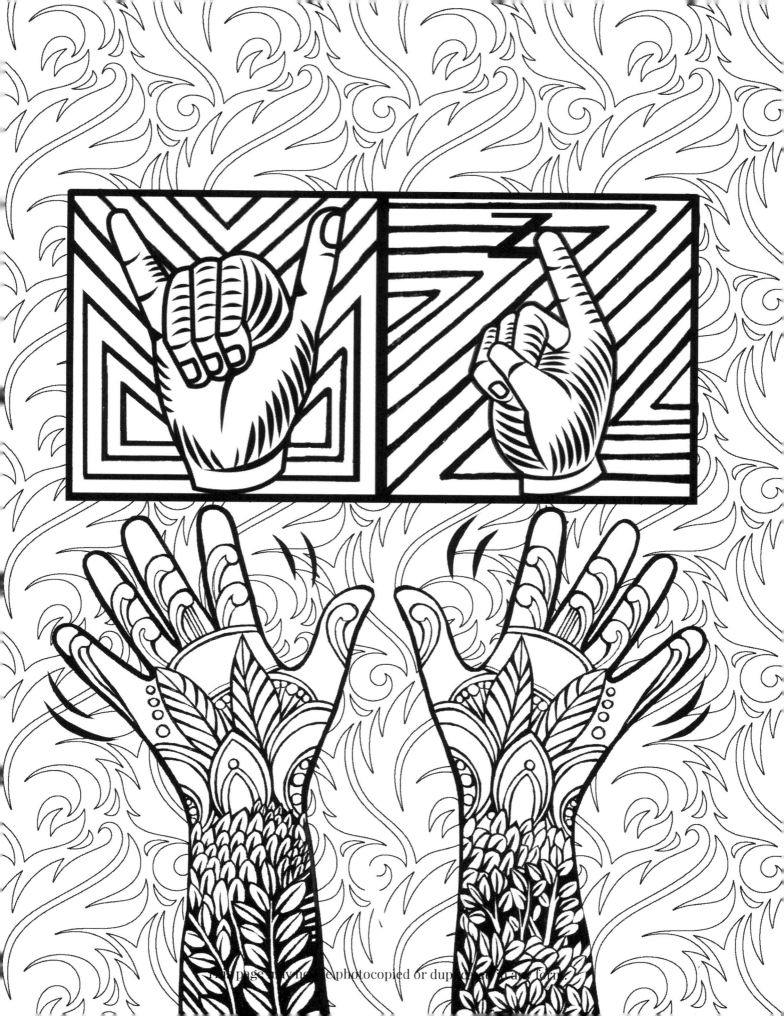

Made in the USA
Middletown, DE
08 July 2017